49erology
Trivia
Challenge

San Francisco 49ers Football

**49erology Trivia Challenge – San Francisco 49ers Football;
First Edition 2008**

Published by
Kick The Ball, Ltd
8595 Columbus Pike, Suite 197
Lewis Center, OH 43035
www.TriviaGameBooks.com

Designed, Formatted, and Edited by: Tom P. Rippey III & Paul F. Wilson
Researched by: Maryzabel C. Rippey

For information on ordering this book in bulk at reduced prices, please email us at pfwilson@trivianthology.com.

International Standard Book Number: 978-1-934372-50-0

Printed & Bound in the United States of America

Tom P. Rippey III & Paul F. Wilson

49erology
Trivia
Challenge

San Francisco 49ers Football

Researched by: Maryzabel C. Rippey

Tom P. Rippey III & Paul F. Wilson, Editors

Kick The Ball, Ltd
Lewis Center, Ohio

This book is dedicated to our families and friends for your unwavering love, support, and your understanding of our pursuit of our passions. Thank you for everything you do for us and for making our lives complete.

Dear Friend,

Thank you for purchasing our *49erology Trivia Challenge* game book!

We hope you enjoy it as much as we enjoyed researching and putting it together. This book can be used over and over again in many different ways. One example would be to use it in a head-to-head challenge by alternating questions between 49er football fans – or by playing as teams. Another option would be to simply challenge yourself to see how many questions you could answer correctly. No matter how you choose to use this book, you'll have fun and maybe even learn a fact or two about 49ers football.

We have made every attempt to verify the accuracy of the questions and answers contained in this book. However it is still possible that from time to time an error has been made by us or our researchers. In the event you find a question or answer that is questionable or inaccurate, we ask for your understanding and thank you for bringing it to our attention so that we may improve future editions of this book. Please email us at tprippey@trivianthology.com with those observations and comments.

Have fun playing *49erology Trivia Challenge*!

Tom & Paul

Tom Rippey & Paul Wilson
Co-Founders, Kick The Ball, Ltd

PS – You can discover more about all of our current trivia game books by visiting us online at www.TriviaGameBooks.com.

Table of Contents

49EROLOGY TRIVIA CHALLENGE

How to Play

Book Format:

There are four quarters, each made up of fifty questions. Each quarter's questions have assigned point values. Questions are designed to get progressively more difficult as you proceed through each quarter, as well as through the book itself. Most questions are in a four-option multiple-choice format so that you will at least have a 25% chance of getting a correct answer for some of the more challenging questions.

We've even added an *Overtime* section in the event of a tie, or just in case you want to keep playing a little longer.

Game Options:

One Player -
To play on your own, simply answer each of the questions in all the quarters, and in the overtime section, if you'd like. Use the *Player / Team Score Sheet* to record your answers and the quarter *Answer Keys* to check your answers. Calculate each quarter's points and the total for the game at the bottom of the *Player / Team Score Sheet* to determine your final score.

Two or More Players –
To play with multiple players decide if you will all be competing with each other individually, or if you will form and play as teams. Each player / team will then have its own *Player / Team Score Sheet* to record its answer. You can use the quarter *Answer Keys* to check your answers and to calculate your final scores.

1

The *Player / Team Score Sheets* have been designed so that each team can answer all questions or you can divide the questions up in any combination you would prefer. For example, you may want to alternate questions if two players are playing or answer every third question for three players, etc. In any case, simply record your response to your questions in the corresponding quarter and question number on the *Player / Team Score Sheet*.

A winner will be determined by multiplying the total number of correct answers for each quarter by the point value per quarter, then adding together the final total for all quarters combined. Play the game again and again by alternating the questions that your team is assigned so that you will answer a different set of questions each time you play.

You Create the Game -
There are countless other ways of using **49erology Trivia Challenge** questions. It's limited only to your imagination. Examples might be using them at your tailgate or other pro football related party. Players / Teams who answer questions incorrectly may have to perform a required action, or winners may receive special prizes. Let us know what other games you come up with!

Have fun!

49EROLOGY TRIVIA CHALLENGE

1) What type of business did the original owners of the 49ers have?

    A) Groceries
    B) Lumber
    C) Mining
    D) Architecture

2) What are the 49ers' official colors?

    A) Velvet Red and Midnight Black
    B) Midnight Black and Metallic Gold
    C) Cardinal Red and Metallic Gold
    D) Metallic Gold and Snow White

3) The 49ers' stadium has a seating capacity of over 70,000.

    A) True
    B) False

4) What year did San Francisco play its first game?

    A) 1946
    B) 1950
    C) 1952
    D) 1956

SAN FRANCISCO 49ERS FOOTBALL

5) Which was NOT one of Joe Montana's nicknames?

A) Joe Cool
B) Big Sky
C) The Comeback Kid
D) The Genius

6) In which division do the 49ers play?

A) AFC South
B) NFC West
C) AFC West
D) NFC South

7) What is the name of the 49ers fight song?

A) Football Polka
B) All The Way
C) Victory March
D) Nasty D

8) How many times did the 49ers play the College All-Stars?

A) 0
B) 3
C) 5
D) 7

First Quarter

49EROLOGY TRIVIA CHALLENGE

9) Who did the 49ers draft with their one and only "Bonus Choice" pick?

    A) Leo Nomellini
    B) Hugh McElhenny
    C) Harry Babcock
    D) Bernie Faloney

10) In what year was the first Bill Walsh Award given?

    A) 1994
    B) 1997
    C) 2001
    D) 2004

11) Who was the last 49er head coach to win NFL Coach of the Year?

    A) Red Hickey
    B) Dick Nolan
    C) Ken Meyer
    D) Bill Walsh

12) Which team has never beaten the 49ers in San Francisco?

    A) New England Patriots
    B) Washington Redskins
    C) Chicago Bears
    D) New York Giants

SAN FRANCISCO 49ERS FOOTBALL

13) Which was NEVER a name of a 49ers stadium?

    A) 3 com
    B) Monster Park
    C) McAfee Coliseum
    D) Kezar Stadium

14) In what year did Ohio businessman Eddie DeBartolo Jr. purchase the 49ers from the original owners?

    A) 1974
    B) 1977
    C) 1979
    D) 1980

15) In what year did the 49ers start to play at Candlestick?

    A) 1955
    B) 1961
    C) 1965
    D) 1971

16) How many times did the 49ers play a Monday Night Football game in 2007?

    A) 0
    B) 1
    C) 2
    D) 3

First Quarter

17) What is the name of San Francisco's mascot?

    A) Bucking Bruce
    B) Sourdough Sam
    C) Goldie
    D) Melvin the Miner

18) When was the last year the 49ers drafted two players from the same school?

    A) 1996
    B) 2000
    C) 2004
    D) 2007

19) Who holds the 49ers career rushing record?

    A) Garrison Hearst
    B) Ken Willard
    C) Roger Craig
    D) Joe Perry

20) Which 49ers player was named NFL Rookie of the Week in 2007?

    A) Joe Staley
    B) Patrick Willis
    C) Jason Hill
    D) Ray McDonald

21) Did Joe Montana win his first game as a starter for the 49ers?

    A) Yes
    B) No

22) What was the name of the formation created by Head Coach Red Hickey in 1960?

    A) Shotgun
    B) Wishbone
    C) T-formation
    D) Five wide receiver set

23) Which 49er head coach has the most wins in a regular season?

    A) Lawrence "Buck" Shaw
    B) Jack Christiansen
    C) Dick Nolan
    D) Bill Walsh

24) In what round was Joe Montana chosen in the NFL Draft?

    A) First
    B) Second
    C) Third
    D) Fourth

25) Who holds the 49ers record for passing yards in a single game?

    A) Joe Montana
    B) Steve Young
    C) Jeff Garcia
    D) John Brodie

26) Who was the first 49ers player to be inducted into the Hall of Fame?

    A) Joe Perry
    B) Hugh McElhenny
    C) Leo Nomellini
    D) John Henry Johnson

27) How many times have the 49ers played in the Super Bowl?

    A) 2
    B) 4
    C) 5
    D) 7

28) What year did the "SF" logo first appear on the helmet?

    A) 1950
    B) 1958
    C) 1960
    D) 1962

49EROLOGY TRIVIA CHALLENGE

29) Do the 49ers have a winning record against the Cowboys in the playoffs?

    A) Yes
    B) No

30) Who was the last player to have gain more than 1,500 total yards for the 49ers in one season?

    A) Ken Willard
    B) Wendell Tyler
    C) Roger Craig
    D) Garrison Hearst

31) Who led the 49ers in sacks during the 2007 regular season?

    A) Joe Cohen
    B) Bryant Young
    C) Marques Douglas
    D) Ronald Fields

32) Which team has San Francisco played the most in postseason games?

    A) Minnesota Vikings
    B) Green Bay Packers
    C) New York Giants
    D) Chicago Bears

33) What are the most regular season wins the 49ers have had in a single season?

    A) 12
    B) 13
    C) 15
    D) 16

34) Which 49er holds the NFL record for most consecutive games with a recorded sack?

    A) Kevin Greene
    B) Chris Doleman
    C) Tommy Hart
    D) Tim Harris

35) Who was the first 49er to finish his career with more than 50 interceptions?

    A) Dave Baker
    B) Kermit Alexander
    C) Jimmy Johnson
    D) Ronnie Lott

36) What single season NFL record did the 49ers set in 1984?

    A) Most consecutive games won with defeat
    B) Most shutout games won or tied in a season
    C) Most games won in a season
    D) Most consecutive home games won

37) Who is the play-by-play announcer for the *Samsung 49ers Radio Network*?

    A) Joe Starkey
    B) Kevin Harlan
    C) Greg Papa
    D) Jon Miller

38) Steve Young has more career completions with the 49ers than Joe Montana.

    A) True
    B) False

39) In the lyrics of the 49ers fight song, "our gang shall" what?

    A) "Go marching to victory"
    B) "Make our joy supreme"
    C) "Put up a fight with might"
    D) "Drive and keep on rolling"

40) Where did Joe Montana play college football?

    A) Texas
    B) Penn State
    C) Notre Dame
    D) Ohio State

49EROLOGY TRIVIA CHALLENGE

41) Which team had the 49ers never beaten at Candlestick until 1981?

A) Rams
B) Bears
C) Vikings
D) Cowboys

42) Who holds the 49ers record for career receptions?

A) Dwight Clark
B) Roger Craig
C) Terrell Owens
D) Jerry Rice

43) What year was the famous "Catch" between Joe Montana and Dwight Clark?

A) 1980
B) 1982
C) 1985
D) 1989

44) Has San Francisco ever lost a Super Bowl?

A) Yes
B) No

49EROLOGY TRIVIA CHALLENGE

45) Which 49er holds the team's single game rushing record?

    A)   Delvin Williams
    B)   Garrison Hearst
    C)   Charlie Garner
    D)   Maurice Hicks

46) Who was the last 49er to win Super Bowl MVP?

    A)   Jerry Rice
    B)   Steve Young
    C)   Joe Montana
    D)   Roger Craig

47) How many one-season head coaches have the 49ers officially had?

    A)   3
    B)   5
    C)   6
    D)   8

48) Did Bill Walsh coach another NFL team after leaving the 49ers?

    A)   Yes
    B)   No

49) Who holds the 49ers record for points scored in a career?

    A) Ray Wersching
    B) Tommy Davis
    C) Mike Cofer
    D) Jerry Rice

50) In which year did the 49ers first celebrate a victory over Dallas?

    A) 1955
    B) 1958
    C) 1960
    D) 1962

First Quarter 49er Cool Fact

The 49ers original team logo and mascot would be considered wild by today's standards. The logo featured a goldminer firing a pair of pistols. The miner appeared to narrowly miss shooting his head and foot. The original logo and mascot was taken from a design off of a railway freight car. In 2006, the mascot's appearance was changed. He used to have a scruffy brown beard, brown eyes, and a wide-brimmed ten-gallon hat with a piece missing from its brim. He now is a clean-shaven goldminer with blue eyes and a hat without any imperfections. He is mainly known as Sourdough Sam but he also has six other nicknames: Sam, Sammy, Samster, Sammiester, Samarama, and Samalamadingdong.

First Quarter Answer Key

1) B – Lumber (The 49ers were started by Tony Morabito and his partners in the lumber business.)

2) C – Cardinal Red and Metallic Gold

3) B – False (Candlestick Park has a seating capacity of 69,732.)

4) A – 1946 (On August 24th as a member of the All-America Football Conference. They won an exhibition game 17-7 against the Los Angeles Dons at Balboa Park in San Diego.)

5) D – The Genius (Actually this was Bill Walsh's nickname for his creative schemes that became known as the West Coast Offense.)

6) B – NFC West (Along with the Arizona Cardinals, Seattle Seahawks, and St. Louis Rams.)

7) A – Football Polka (Composed by Martin Judnich in 1952.)

8) A – 0 (The NFL Champion played the College All-Stars for 41 years starting in 1934. The 49ers never won an NFL Championship during this period.)

9) C – Harry Babcock (The bonus choice was essentially the #1 overall pick of the draft and was used by the NFL from 1947-58. The 49ers won the draw in 1953 and choose Georgia end, Harry Babcock.)

10) D – 2004 (This award is voted on by coaches only and is given to the 49ers' team MVP. It was last awarded to CB Nate Clements and LB Patrick Willis in 2007.)

11) D – Bill Walsh (1981)

12) A – New England Patriots (The 49ers are 4-0 at home against the Patriots.)

13) C – McAfee Coliseum (This is actually the name of the team across the bay, the Oakland Raiders.)

14) B – 1977 (DeBartolo of Youngstown, Ohio, emerged to buy the franchise from the wives of the original owners. Immediately after the purchase he began making changes which included the hiring of now-legendary Head Coach Bill Walsh.)

15) D – 1971 (Ground was broken in 1958 for the new home of the San Francisco Giants, who were moving west from New York. The Giants officially chose the name of Candlestick Park after a name-the-park contest in 1959. In 1971, the 49ers became tenants as well.)

16) C – 2 (The 49ers beat Arizona 20-17 in week 1 and lost to Seattle 0-24 in week 10.)

17) B – Sourdough Sam (The original goldminer idea came from one of Morabito's partners in the lumber business.)

18) D – 2007 (With two choices from Florida, DE Ray McDonald in the 3rd round and DT Joe Cohen in the 4th round.)

19) D – Joe Perry (7,344 yards rushing from 1950-60, 1963)

20) B – Patrick Willis (In 2007 this linebacker was the Rookie of the Week in week 1 with 11 tackles and a forced fumble, week 2 with eight tackles, week 12 with 18 tackles and ½ sack and week 16 with 20 tackles, two sacks and one forced fumble.)

21) B – No (Montana lost 10-13 vs. the St. Louis Cardinals in 1979.)

22) A – Shotgun (The 49ers were the first to use this formation in 1960 in a game against the Baltimore Colts.)

23) D – Bill Walsh (Career record of 102-63-1)

24) C – Third (Montana was a 3rd round draft choice in 1979.)

25) A – Joe Montana (In 1990 Montana threw for 476 yards against Atlanta.)

26) C – Leo Nomellini (Nicknamed "The Lion", he was the 49ers first draft choice in 1950 and inducted into the Pro Football Hall of Fame in 1969.)

27) C – 5 (Super Bowls XVI, XIX, XXIII, XXIV, and XXIX)

28) D – 1962 (The black outlining of the SF was added in 1989 and the black border with gold trimming around the oval was added in 1996.)

29) B – No (Current record is 2-5 against the Cowboys for a .286 winning percentage.)

30) D – Garrison Hearst (1,570 yards in 1998)

31) B – Bryant Young (Young recorded 6 ½ sacks during the regular season.)

32) C – New York Giants (7 times with a record of 4-3: 1981 [38-24], 1984 [21-10], 1985 [3-17], 1986 [3-49], 1990 [13-15], 1993 [44-3], and 2002 [39-38])

33) C – 15 (In 1984, the 49ers went 15-1 with their only loss to the Steelers [17-20].)

34) A – Kevin Greene (In 1997 he had 9 consecutive games with recorded sacks.)

35) D – Ronnie Lott (From 1981-90 he had 51 interceptions. In 2000 he was inducted into the Pro Football Hall of Fame.)

36) C – Most games won in a season (This record was set in 1984 and has since been broken by New England after going 16-0 in 2007.)

37) A – Joe Starkey (Since 1989.)

38) B – False (Montana 2,929 career completions and Young has 2,400.)

39) D – "Drive and keep on rolling" (The actual line from the *Football Polka* is "Our gang shall drive and keep on rolling, And across the goal they'll go".)

40) C – Notre Dame (True to form, Montana led the Fighting Irish to two consecutive fourth quarter comeback wins in his first two games. His last game as a collegiate is known as the "Chicken Soup Game" in which he led Notre Dame to a fourth quarter Cotton Bowl victory while ill.)

41) A – Rams (With a score of 20-17. Before this victory, the Rams had won 24 of the 27 previous meetings.)

42) D – Jerry Rice (From 1985-2000, he had 1,281 receptions.)

43) B – 1982 (This play went down in 49ers history on January 10, 1982. During this nail-biting NFC Championship game Montana's game-ending pass would win the game against the Dallas Cowboys with a score of 28-27.)

44) B – No (The 49ers are the only team to have played in more than one Super Bowl and to have never lost.)

45) C – Charlie Garner (201 yards against Dallas in 2000.)

46) B – Steve Young (As quarterback in Super Bowl XXIX.)

47) B – 5 (The five coaches were Strader 1955, Clark 1976, Meyer 1977, McCulley 1978, and O'Connor 1978. The last two shared a season with McCulley coaching the first 9 games and O'Connor coaching the final 7 games.)

48) B – No (Walsh did not continue with the NFL, but he did go on to coach for the Stanford Cardinals from 1992-94.)

49) D – Jerry Rice (1,130 career points scored from 1985-2000: 187 TDs and 4 2-PT conversions.)

50) C – 1960 (The 49ers won 26-14 at Dallas.)

Note: All answers valid as of the end of the 2007 season, unless otherwise indicated in the question itself.

Second Quarter *2-Point Questions*

1) Who is San Francisco's practice facility named after?

   A) The owner's daughter
   B) The owner's dog
   C) The owner's sister
   D) The owner's mother

2) What number did Jerry Rice wear while playing with San Francisco?

   A) 80
   B) 81
   C) 87
   D) 89

3) When was the last time the 49ers drafted a running back in the first round?

   A) 1984
   B) 1988
   C) 1990
   D) 1994

4) Which decade did the 49ers have the best winning percentage (including postseason)?

   A) 1940s
   B) 1950s
   C) 1980s
   D) 1990s

Second Quarter *2-Point Questions*

5) Do the 49ers have an all-time winning record against the Rams?

    A) Yes
    B) No

6) What is the 49ers record for most consecutive 10-win seasons?

    A) 7
    B) 9
    C) 13
    D) 16

7) What are the most rushing yards for the 49ers in a Super Bowl?

    A) 181
    B) 195
    C) 211
    D) 220

8) Where did Jerry Rice play college football?

    A) Mississippi Valley State University
    B) University of Mississippi
    C) Louisiana State University
    D) Tulane University

9) Which 49ers' quarterback was a lefty?

    A) Joe Montana
    B) Ken Dorsey
    C) Elvis Grbac
    D) Steve Young

10) How many teams have the 49ers played 50 or more times in the regular season?

    A) 4
    B) 6
    C) 8
    D) 10

11) What are the most points the 49ers have allowed in a playoff game?

    A) 38
    B) 41
    C) 49
    D) 55

12) Against which team was the 49ers first NFL win?

    A) Chicago Bears
    B) Detroit Lions
    C) Green Bay Packers
    D) Baltimore Colts

13) Does Steve Young have more career passing attempts than Joe Montana?

    A) Yes
    B) No

14) When was the last time a player gained over 200 yards rushing in a game against the 49ers?

    A) 1996
    B) 1999
    C) 2006
    D) Never

15) What is the record for longest field goal kicked by a 49er at home?

    A) 48
    B) 50
    C) 54
    D) 58

16) Which of the following 49ers led the league in scoring?

    A) Ray Wersching
    B) Jerry Rice
    C) Gordy Soltau
    D) Mike Cofer

17) For how many seasons did Steve Young lead the league in touchdowns?

    A) 1
    B) 2
    C) 3
    D) 4

18) When was the last time the 49ers had over 500 yards of total offense?

    A) 1992
    B) 1996
    C) 2000
    D) 2003

19) How many times has San Francisco had the number one overall draft pick?

    A) 1
    B) 3
    C) 4
    D) 6

20) San Francisco was Bill Walsh's first head coaching position in the NFL.

    A) True
    B) False

21) How many yards is the longest rushing play in San Francisco history?

  A) 88
  B) 91
  C) 96
  D) 99

22) Which team has San Francisco never beaten at home?

  A) Atlanta Falcons
  B) Kansas City Chiefs
  C) Jacksonville Jaguars
  D) New York Jets

23) Who was the first running back to gain more than 1,000 yards rushing and 1,000 yards receiving in the same season?

  A) Dexter Carter
  B) Roger Craig
  C) Garrison Hearst
  D) Kermit Johnson

24) How many times have the 49ers played in the NFC Wild Card Playoff Game?

  A) 1
  B) 2
  C) 4
  D) 5

25) The 49ers have NEVER been outgained in any Super Bowl appearance.

    A) True
    B) False

26) In what year did the 49ers win their first playoff game?

    A) 1957
    B) 1960
    C) 1963
    D) 1970

27) How many times has San Francisco lost a home opener?

    A) 19
    B) 22
    C) 25
    D) 28

28) Who is the only San Francisco player NOT to be named NFL Defensive Rookie of the Year?

    A) Charles Haley
    B) Bruce Taylor
    C) Dana Stubblefield
    D) Patrick Willis

29) How many years did Roger Craig play football for the 49ers?

- A) 5
- B) 7
- C) 8
- D) 10

30) How many games did the 49ers play in their first NFL season?

- A) 6
- B) 8
- C) 12
- D) 15

31) What is the San Francisco record for the longest punt?

- A) 80 yards
- B) 85 yards
- C) 90 yards
- D) 95 yards

32) Do the 49ers have an all-time winning record against the AFC?

- A) Yes
- B) No

33) Who was the last 49er to have over 100 receptions in a single season?

    A) Roger Craig
    B) Terrell Owens
    C) Jerry Rice
    D) Dwight Clark

34) Who is the only 49er running back to have rushed for over 200 yards in a single game?

    A) Garrison Hearst
    B) Delvin Williams
    C) Charlie Garner
    D) Hugh McElhenny

35) To which team did San Francisco suffer its worst loss in its first NFL season?

    A) Cleveland Browns
    B) Los Angeles Rams
    C) Detroit Lions
    D) Chicago Bears

36) Who was the 49ers' first opponent at Candlestick?

    A) Los Angeles Rams
    B) New Orleans Saints
    C) Philadelphia Eagles
    D) Chicago Bears

37) For how many yards was the longest touchdown drive by the 49ers in 2007?

    A) 72
    B) 79
    C) 82
    D) 88

38) Which 49er has played in the most Pro Bowls?

    A) Bob St. Clair
    B) Ronnie Lott
    C) Leo Nomellini
    D) Jimmy Johnson

39) Who holds the San Francisco record for passing yards in a season?

    A) Steve Young
    B) Jeff Garcia
    C) Joe Montana
    D) John Brodie

40) San Francisco has an all-time winning record against every NFL North opponent.

    A) True
    B) False

41) Who holds the 49ers record for receiving yards in a single game during the regular season?

- A) John Taylor
- B) Jerry Rice
- C) Terrell Owens
- D) Dwight Clark

42) Who was the last quarterback to start for San Francisco before Joe Montana began his streak?

- A) Scott Bull
- B) Jim Plunkett
- C) Steve DeBerg
- D) Norm Snead

43) When was the last time a 49er returned a fumble for a touchdown?

- A) 1992
- B) 1996
- C) 1999
- D) 2005

44) How many times have San Francisco head coaches been named NFL Coach of the Year?

- A) 5
- B) 6
- C) 7
- D) 9

45) Did Steve Young have more than 30,000 career passing yards?

    A) Yes
    B) No

46) Who holds the San Francisco record for career sacks?

    A) Fred Dean
    B) Bryant Young
    C) Tommy Hart
    D) Cedrick Hardman

47) How many times did Jerry Rice gain over 1,500 yards receiving in a single season while at San Francisco?

    A) 1
    B) 3
    C) 4
    D) Never

48) When was the last time the Niners had a punt blocked?

    A) 1992
    B) 1996
    C) 1999
    D) 2005

49EROLOGY TRIVIA CHALLENGE

49) In how many different decades have the 49ers won at least 85 games?

    A) 1
    B) 2
    C) 3
    D) 4

50) Which Super Bowl was Jerry Rice voted MVP?

    A) XVI
    B) XIX
    C) XXIII
    D) XXIX

Second Quarter 49er Cool Fact

The point and cove on the San Francisco Bay in which the ballpark was built was given its name from the indigenous candlestick bird. These birds were hunted for their delicate meat and were extinct by the 1950s. The stadium was originally built for the San Francisco Giants and the 49ers have been sole tenants since 2000. The stadium survived the 1989 San Francisco earthquake relatively unscathed. The name of the stadium has changed various times since naming rights were first sold in 1995. However, in June of 2008 the name of the stadium will once again be officially known as Candlestick Park.

Second Quarter Answer Key

1) D – The owner's mother (The Marie P. DeBartolo Sports Centre in Santa Clara, CA, is named after the mother of former owner, Eddie Bartolo,Jr. and current owner, Denise Bartolo York.)

2) A – 80 (Rice wore #80 with the 49ers from 1985-2000.)

3) C – 1990 (The 49ers took Dexter Carter, Florida State, with the 25th overall pick.)

4) A – 1940s (The 49ers went 39-15-2 for a .732 winning percentage.)

5) B – No (The 49ers are 56-60-2 [.483] against the Rams.)

6) D – 16 (The 49ers went 10-16 in 1983, 15-1 in 1984, 10-6 in 1985, 10-5-1 in 1986, 13-2 in 1987, 10-6 in 1988, 14-2 in 1989, 14-2 in 1990, 10-6 in 1991, 14-2 in 1992, 10-6 in 1993, 13-3 in 1994, 11-5 in 1995, 12-4 in 1996, 13-3 in 1997, and 12-4 in 1998)

7) C – 211 (Super Bowl XIX vs. Miami)

8) A – Mississippi Valley State University (Rice attended from 1981-85. He acquired the nickname 'World' since there was not a ball in the world he could not catch. Their football stadium is named in his honor.)

9) D – Steve Young (In 2005 Steve Young became the first lefty QB to be inducted into the Pro Football Hall of Fame.)

10) B – 6 (The 49ers have played six teams more than 50 times: Packers [54], Bears [57], Lions [59], Saints [69], Falcons [72], and Rams [116].)

11) C – 49 (The 49ers lost 3-49 to the New York Giants in the 1986 NFC Divisional Playoff.)

12) B – Detroit Lions (The 49ers beat the Lions 28-27 in 1950.)

13) B – No (Joe Montana has 4,600 career passing attempts [1979-92] and Steve Young has 3,648 [1987-99].)

14) D – Never (San Francisco's defense has never allowed a running back to gain over 200 yards.)

15) C – 54 (By Bruce Gossett vs. New Orleans in 1973.)

16) C – Gordy Soltau (Soltau led the league in 1952-53.)

17) D – 4 (Young led the league in touchdowns in 1992-94, 1998.)

18) D – 2003 (The 49ers gained 502 yards against Cincinnati.)

19) B – 3 (The 49ers drafted Harry Babcock from Georgia in 1953, Dave Parks from Texas Tech in 1964, and Alex Smith from Utah in 2005.)

20) A – True (At the age of 47 Walsh became a head coach of an NFL team for the first time. He spent 10 seasons with the 49ers.)

21) C – 96 (Garrison Hearst had a 96-yard touchdown run against the Jets in 1998 which led to a 36-30 win in overtime.)

22) C – Jacksonville Jaguars (The 49ers have never hosted the Jaguars at home. They have met twice and have a losing record against the Jaguars, 1994 [3-41] and 2005 [9-10].)

23) B – Roger Craig (In 1985 Craig achieved this feat by gaining 1,050 yards rushing and 1,016 yards receiving.)

24) D – 5 (The 49ers are 3-2 al- time in Wild Card Playoff games [1985, 1996, 1998, 2001, and 2002].)

25) B – False (The 49ers were outgained 88 yards by the Bengals in Super Bowl XVI.)

26) D – 1970 (San Francisco played the Vikings in the NFC Divisional Playoff winning the game 17-14.)

27) C – 25 (Since 1946 the 49ers are 35-25-2 [.581] in home openers.)

28) A – Charles Haley (Haley was a linebacker for the 49ers from 1986-91, 1999.)

29) B – 7 (While with the Niners Craig caught a then-record 92 passes in 1985 and set a then-franchise record 1,502 yards rushing in 1988.)

30) C – 12 (The 49ers finished 3-9 in 1950.)

31) D – 95 yards (John Taylor had a 95-yarder against Washington in 1988.)

32) A – Yes (San Francisco has an all-time record of 96-90 against the AFC for a .516 winning percentage.)

33) C – Jerry Rice (Rice accomplished this feat three times with 108 receptions in 1996, 122 in 1995, and 112 in 1994.)

34) C – Charlie Garner (He had 36 carries for 201 yards against Dallas in 2000.)

35) B – Los Angeles Rams (San Francisco lost 14-35 to the Rams in 1950.)

36) A – Los Angeles Rams (The 49ers lost their first game at Candlestick vs. the Rams 13-20 in 1971.)

37) D – 88 (Arnaz Battle caught a 57-yard pass from Trent Dilfer for the touchdown.)

38) C – Leo Nomellini (Nomellini played for the 49ers from 1950-63. He made the Pro Bowl 10 times [1950-53, 1956-61].)

39) B – Jeff Garcia (Garcia passed for 4,278 yards in 2000.)

40) B – False (The 49ers have a .853 winning percentage against the Bengals and a .539 against the Lions.)

41) B – Jerry Rice (Rice gained 289 yards against the Vikings in 1995.)

42) C – Steve DeBerg (DeBerg played for the Niners from 1978-80. He was the first significant West Coast Offense quarterback under Bill Walsh.)

43) D – 2005 (In 2005, both Derek Smith and Derrick Johnson recovered fumbles for 2 touchdowns against Arizona.)

44) A – 5 (Howard 'Red' Hickey in 1959, Bill Walsh in 1981, and George Seifert in 1989, 1990, & 1994.)

45) B – No (Young has 29,907 career passing yards.)

46) D – Cedrick Hardman (Hardman had 112.5 career sacks [1970-79].)

47) B – 3 (Rice has accomplished this feat in three single seasons with 1,503 yards in 1993, 1,570 yards in 1986, and 1,848 yards in 1995.)

48) D – 2005 (Arizona blocked Keith Lewis's punt in 2005.)

49) B – 2 (San Francisco won 104 games in the '80s and 113 in the '90s.)

50) C – XXIII (This is the only 49er Super Bowl in which a quarterback did not win MVP.)

Note: All answers valid as of the end of the 2007 season, unless otherwise indicated in the question itself.

49EROLOGY TRIVIA CHALLENGE

1) Since 1970, how many times has San Francisco lost in the NFC Championship game?

    A) 2
    B) 3
    C) 5
    D) 7

2) Steve Young holds the Super Bowl record for most touchdown passes in a single game?

    A) True
    B) False

3) Since 1946, which year was San Francisco's first 10-win season?

    A) 1948
    B) 1953
    C) 1956
    D) 1960

4) Which 49ers head coach has the second most wins while at San Francisco?

    A) George Seifert
    B) Buck Shaw
    C) Steve Mariucci
    D) Bill Walsh

5) What is the largest margin of victory for the 49ers in a playoff game?

    A) 24
    B) 28
    C) 32
    D) 39

6) Who holds the 49ers' career record for receiving yards?

    A) Jerry Rice
    B) Terrell Owens
    C) Dwight Clark
    D) John Taylor

7) What famous college football coach was drafted by the 49ers in 1967 as their first round draft choice?

    A) Steve Spurrier
    B) Barry Alvarez
    C) Tom Osborne
    D) Pete Carroll

8) How many combined kickoffs and punts were returned for touchdowns by the 49ers in 2007?

    A) 0
    B) 1
    C) 2
    D) 4

9) What is the San Francisco record for PATs made in a single game?

- A) 5
- B) 7
- C) 8
- D) 10

10) In which decade did the 49ers fail to have a 10-win season?

- A) 1940s
- B) 1950s
- C) 1960s
- D) 1970s

11) Joe Montana once threw 4 touchdowns in a single quarter.

- A) True
- B) False

12) How many interceptions has Joe Montana thrown in his Super Bowl career?

- A) 0
- B) 2
- C) 5
- D) 8

13) Since 1982, how many times has a linebacker led the 49ers in sacks?

    A) 5
    B) 6
    C) 8
    D) 11

14) Who is the only 49er defender to have recorded 4 interceptions in a single game?

    A) Ronnie Heard
    B) Dave Baker
    C) Rod Woodson
    D) Eric Wright

15) Which 49ers coach has the best winning percentage? (Minimum 3 seasons)

    A) George Seifert
    B) Bill Walsh
    C) Buck Shaw
    D) Steve Mariucci

16) What is the San Francisco record for highest total offense in a single game?

    A) 563
    B) 579
    C) 598
    D) 612

17) Who was the last San Francisco player to record over 150 tackles in a single season?

A) Patrick Willis
B) Derek Smith
C) Jeff Ulbrich
D) Ken Norton, Jr

18) What is the 49er record for most consecutive losses?

A) 5
B) 6
C) 9
D) 12

19) When was the last time the season leading passer for San Francisco had less than 1,000 yards passing?

A) 1998
B) 2000
C) 2005
D) 2007

20) Who was the last receiver to lead the 49ers in scoring?

A) Jerry Rice
B) Delvin Williams
C) Terrell Owens
D) Ken Willard

49EROLOGY TRIVIA CHALLENGE

21) What is San Francisco's winning percentage at home?

A) .574
B) .601
C) .632
D) .667

22) What is the name of San Francisco's official cheerleaders?

A) The Gold Rush
B) The Miners
C) The Rushers
D) The Goldies

23) Who was the last 49er to have his number retired?

A) Dwight Clark
B) Joe Montana
C) Bob St. Clair
D) Ronnie Lott

24) When was the last time the 49ers gained over 2,500 rushing yards as a team in a single season?

A) 1971
B) 1987
C) 1998
D) 2004

25) Steve Young and Joe Montana combined for over 1,000 career pass attempts in 49ers playoff games.

  A) True
  B) False

26) Against which team did San Francisco go into overtime in 2007?

  A) Arizona Cardinal
  B) St. Louis Rams
  C) Pittsburg Steelers
  D) Baltimore Ravens

27) Who was the first San Francisco player to be named NFC Rookie of the Year?

  A) Ronnie Lott
  B) Bruce Taylor
  C) Jerry Rice
  D) Bryant Young

28) Since 1970, how many times has a non-kicker led the 49ers in scoring?

  A) 2
  B) 4
  C) 5
  D) 7

29) In which year did San Francisco get their 500 all-time win?

    A) 1999
    B) 2004
    C) 2006
    D) 2007

30) What is the combined winning percentage for coaches who lasted only one season at San Francisco?

    A) .339
    B) .401
    C) .432
    D) .467

31) In how many regular season games did a 49er running back rush for more than 100 yards in 2007?

    A) 0
    B) 2
    C) 4
    D) 8

32) What is San Francisco's longest drought between playoff appearances since 1950?

    A) 5 years
    B) 7 years
    C) 10 years
    D) 14 years

Third Quarter   *3-Point Questions*

33) Against which AFC team does San Francisco have the best all-time winning percentage (min. 3 games)?

    A) Baltimore Ravens
    B) New York Jets
    C) Cincinnati Bengals
    D) Indianapolis Colts

34) How did San Francisco score its first points in Super Bowl XVI?

    A) Punt return
    B) Receiving touchdown
    C) Field goal
    D) Rushing touchdown

35) Has San Francisco ever failed to rush for 1,000 yards as a team in a season?

    A) Yes
    B) No

36) Which San Francisco quarterback has the most consecutive games with 300 yards passing?

    A) Steve DeBerg
    B) Jeff Garcia
    C) Steve Young
    D) Joe Montana

49EROLOGY TRIVIA CHALLENGE

37) Who was the first round pick for the 49ers in the 2008 NFL Draft?

- A) Kentwan Balmer
- B) Reggie Smith
- C) Chilo Rachal
- D) Cody Wallace

38) Has any 49er player ever led the team in rushing and passing in the same year?

- A) Yes
- B) No

39) Who scored San Francisco's final TD in Super Bowl XXIX?

- A) William Floyd
- B) Ricky Watters
- C) Jerry Rice
- D) Adam Walker

40) Which famous running back finished his career with the 49ers?

- A) Marcus Allen
- B) Eric Dickerson
- C) O.J. Simpson
- D) John Riggins

SAN FRANCISCO 49ERS FOOTBALL

Third Quarter

41) When was the last time the 49ers went undefeated in the preseason?

    A) 1988
    B) 1990
    C) 1992
    D) 1994

42) What was San Francisco's largest margin of victory in 1984?

    A) 28
    B) 32
    C) 38
    D) 44

43) Which of the following San Francisco quarterbacks NEVER threw 5 touchdown passes in a single game?

    A) Joe Montana
    B) Steve Spurrier
    C) John Brodie
    D) Jeff Garcia

44) Who coached San Francisco after Bill Walsh?

    A) Steve Mariucci
    B) George Seifert
    C) Dennis Erickson
    D) Mike Nolan

45) Who scored the only points for the 49ers in the 2002 NFC Divisional Playoff versus the Buccaneers?

A) Jeff Ulbrich
B) Julian Peterson
C) Jeff Chandler
D) Zack Bronson

46) Did Bill Walsh win his last regular season game as 49ers head coach?

A) Yes
B) No

47) Where did the 49ers play their home games before Candlestick?

A) McAfee Coliseum
B) Stanford Stadium
C) Monster Park
D) Kezar Stadium

48) How many receptions did Jerry Rice have his rookie season?

A) 27
B) 38
C) 49
D) 61

49EROLOGY TRIVIA CHALLENGE

49) When was the last time the 49ers led the NFL in rushing defense?

    A) 1989
    B) 1992
    C) 1995
    D) 2001

50) What is the 49er record for most consecutive playoff losses?

    A) 1
    B) 3
    C) 5
    D) 6

Third Quarter 49er Cool Fact

There is no arguing that Joe Montana was a talented quarterback, but he was also a very talented basketball player. He helped his school win the 1973 Pennsylvania AAA Basketball Championship. His senior year he was named to the All-State team. He was offered scholarships to play basketball for North Carolina and North Carolina State. He considered NC State because of the opportunity to also play football for the Wolfpack. However, after being named All-American as a quarterback his senior year, Montana had received offers from many colleges including Notre Dame. The Fighting Irish had the upper hand since Montana's boyhood idol, Terry Hanratty, was a successful quarterback at Notre Dame. In 2006, Montana's old high school renamed their football stadium "Joe Montana Stadium." 49er history would not be the same had Joe chosen the hardcourt instead of the gridiron.

Third Quarter Answer Key

1) D – 7 (The 49ers lost 17-10 to Dallas in 1970, 14-3 to Dallas in 1971, 24-21 to Washington in 1983, 15-13 to the Giants in 1990, 30-20 to Dallas in 1992, 38-21 to Dallas in 1993, and 23-10 to Green Bay in 1997.)

2) A – Steve Young (Young passed for 325 yards and 6 touchdowns in Super Bowl XXIX for a 49-26 win over the Chargers. He was also named MVP.)

3) A – 1948 (The 49ers went 12-2 under Shaw in 1948.)

4) D – Bill Walsh (102 wins from 1979-88)

5) B – 28 (The 49ers beat the Vikings 41-13 in the 1989 NFC Divisional Playoff game.)

6) A – Jerry Rice (He gained 19,247 yards in 16 seasons with San Francisco [1985-2000].)

7) A – Steve Spurrier (Known as the football coach for the University of South Carolina, he played for the 49ers from 1967-75.)

8) A – 0 (In 2007 San Francisco had 56 punt returns and 73 kick returns for 0 touchdowns.)

9) C – 8 (Mike Cofer completed all 8 attempts against Atlanta in 1992.)

10) B – 1950s (The best season during the decade was a 9-3 season in 1953 under Shaw.)

11) A – True (In 1989 Montana threw 4 touchdowns in the 4th quarter to win 38-28 against the Eagles. Montana ended up throwing 425 yards and had a total of 5 touchdowns for this game.)

12) A – 0 (Montana is considered to be the best big game performer ever.)

13) D – 11 (Fred Dean in 1982 & 1983, Charles Haley in 1986, 1987, 1988, 1989, 1990, & 1991, Tim Harris in 1992, Rickey Jackson in 1995, and Julian Peterson in 2003)

14) B – Dave Baker (He pulled down 4 interceptions for a 23-7 win over the Rams in 1960.)

15) B – Bill Walsh (.582 [102-73-1])

16) C – 598 yards (Set against Buffalo in 1992.)

17) A – Patrick Willis (174 tackles in 2007)

18) C – 9 (The 49ers lost 9 straight games in 1978.)

19) C – 2005 (Alex Smith led San Francisco with 875 yards.)

20) C – Terrell Owens (Owens led the team with 14 touchdowns and 84 points in 2002.)

21) B – .601 (The 49ers have an all-time record at home of 270-178-8.)

22) A – The Gold Rush (Founded in 1983, they were named 'The Gold Rush' to commemorate the excitement that brought millions of people to California in search of gold.)

23) D – Ronnie Lott (Lott's #42 was retired in 2003. Lott played for San Francisco from 1981-90.)

24) C – 1998 (The 49ers gained 2,544 yards in 1998. In 1954 they gained 2,498, and in 1988 they gained 2,523 yards.)

25) A – True (Montana had 593 career playoff pass attempts and Young had 471 pass attempts.)

26) A – Arizona Cardinal (The 49ers beat the Cardinal 37-31 at Arizona.)

27) D – Bryant Young (He was given this award in 1994.)

28) B – 4 (Delvin William in 1977, Terrell Owens in 2002, and Jerry Rice in 1987 & 1995.)

29) B – 2004 (The 49ers beat Arizona 31-28 in overtime to get their 500th win.)

30) A – .339 (One year coaches had a combined record of 19-37 with the 49ers.)

31) B – 2 (Frank Gore in week 12 vs. Arizona with 116 yards and in week 15 vs. Cincinnati with 138 yards.)

32) D – 14 years (The 49ers failed to make the playoffs from 1957-1970. The 1960s is the only decade that San Francisco never had a playoff appearance.)

33) B – New York Jets (The 49ers have an all-time record of 8-2 against the Jets.)

34) D – Rushing touchdown (The first score of the game came on a 1-yard quarterback sneak.)

35) A – Yes (The lowest single season rushing yards as a team for the 49ers was 740 yards in 1982.)

36) C – Steve Young (In 1982 Montana would throw for 300 yards in 5 straight games. In 1998 Young broke this record with 6 straight games.)

37) A – Kentwan Balmer (The 49ers took the defensive tackle from UNC.)

38) B – No (Steve Young was the 2nd leading rusher 6 times. He came within 146 yards in 1991 of being leading rusher.)

39) C – Jerry Rice (Rice received a 7-yard toss from Steve Young in the 4th quarter with 1:11 left on the clock which led to a 49-26 win over the Chargers. Rice scored 3 TDs while catching 10 passes for 149 yards. He established career records for receptions, yards, and touchdowns in a Super Bowl.)

40) C – O.J. Simpson (Simpson played with the 49ers from 1978-79.)

41) C – 1992 (San Francisco went 5-0 in preseason, 14-2 during the regular season, and lost in the NFC Championship 20-30 against Dallas.)

42) D – 44 (San Francisco beat Minnesota 51-7 with a 44 point margin of victory.)

43) D – Jeff Garcia (Montana had 2 five-touchdown games, Spurrier had 1, and Brodie had 1. Montana also had 1 six-touchdown game.)

44) B – George Seifert (Seifert was the head coach of the 49ers from 1989-96.)

45) C – Jeff Chandler (In the 31-6 loss to the Buccaneers, Chandler had a 24-yard field goal in the 1st quarter and a 40-yard field goal in the 2nd quarter.)

46) B – No (San Francisco lost to the Los Angeles Rams 16-38 in 1988, but they did go on to win Super Bowl XXIII 20-16 vs. the Bengals.)

47) D – Kezar Stadium (For 24 seasons the 49ers called this stadium home [1946-71].)

48) C – 49 (In his rookie season he recorded 49 catches for 927 yards and an 18.9 yard per catch average.)

49) C – 1995 (San Francisco had 66.3 yards. They also led in Total Defense with 274.9 yards.)

50) B – 3 (The 49ers lost 3 straight with the playoffs in 1985, 1987, and 1988.)

Note: All answers valid as of the end of the 2007 season, unless otherwise indicated in the question itself.

Fourth Quarter *4-Point Questions*

1) When was the last time a 49ers game resulted in a tie?

    A) 1986
    B) 1990
    C) 1996
    D) 2000

2) When was the last time the 49ers were shutout?

    A) 1998
    B) 2000
    C) 2004
    D) 2007

3) How many 49er players have had their numbers retired?

    A) 5
    B) 8
    C) 10
    D) 12

4) Since 1970, has San Francisco ever led the league in rushing offense, passing offense, and total offense in the same year?

    A) Yes
    B) No

Fourth Quarter *4-Point Questions*

5) Which 49er has made the most field goals in a single game?

    A) Jeff Chandler
    B) Bruce Gossett
    C) Jeff Wilkins
    D) Joe Nedney

6) Who was the last 49er head coach to win his first regular season NFL game?

    A) Dick Nolan
    B) Bill Walsh
    C) George Seifert
    D) Steve Mariucci

7) What is the San Francisco record for most consecutive years appearing in the playoffs?

    A) 2
    B) 3
    C) 5
    D) 8

8) How many San Francisco coaches are in the Pro Football Hall of Fame?

    A) 0
    B) 1
    C) 3
    D) 5

Fourth Quarter

49EROLOGY TRIVIA CHALLENGE

9) Against which AFC team does San Francisco have the worst all-time winning percentage (min. 3 games)?

    A) Minnesota
    B) Indianapolis
    C) Baltimore
    D) Cleveland

10) Did Bill Walsh have a winning record when coaching against the Cowboys?

    A) Yes
    B) No

11) Which of the following players WAS NOT named a Consensus All-Pro in 1998?

    A) Ray Brown
    B) Kevin Gogan
    C) Merton Hanks
    D) Garrison Hearst

12) When was the last time the 49ers had two players gain over 100 yards rushing in the same game?

    A) 1995
    B) 2001
    C) 2004
    D) Never had two 100-yard rushers

SAN FRANCISCO 49ERS FOOTBALL

13) In which of the following categories did Mason Crosby lead the NFL in 2007?

   A) Points scored
   B) Field goals made
   C) Extra points made
   D) Field goal percentage

14) Who holds the San Francisco single season rushing record?

   A) Ken Willard
   B) Garrison Hearst
   C) Frank Gore
   D) Jeff Moore

15) Which opponent handed San Francisco its worst defeat in 2007?

   A) New York Giants
   B) Dallas Cowboys
   C) Indianapolis Colts
   D) Seattle Seahawks

16) Joe Montana passed for more than 2,000 yards every season with San Francisco.

   A) True
   B) False

17) What year did an African-American first play for the 49ers?

    A) 1946
    B) 1948
    C) 1955
    D) 1959

18) Which player holds the 49er record for most seasons with over 1,000 yards receiving?

    A) Terrell Owens
    B) John Taylor
    C) Jerry Rice
    D) Gene Washington

19) Who holds the San Francisco records for rushing touchdowns in a game and season?

    A) Roger Craig
    B) Ken Williard
    C) Billy Kilmer
    D) Ricky Waters

20) Which quarterback holds the 49er record for best passing efficiency in his first season as a starter?

    A) Joe Montana
    B) Jeff Garcia
    C) Bob Waters
    D) Steve Young

Fourth Quarter *4-Point Questions*

21) How many head coaches have the 49ers had in their history?

    A) 10
    B) 12
    C) 15
    D) 16

22) What is San Francisco's largest margin of victory over Dallas?

    A) 14
    B) 18
    C) 25
    D) 31

23) Which head coach has the second best winning percentage at San Francisco (min. 3 seasons)?

    A) George Seifert
    B) Steve Mariucci
    C) Buck Shaw
    D) Bill Walsh

24) Has San Francisco played every NFL team at least once?

    A) Yes
    B) No

25) Which 49er player won the Ed Block Courage Award in 2007?

- A) Frank Gore
- B) Eric Heitmann
- C) Walt Harris
- D) Patrick Willis

26) San Francisco has an all-time regular season winning record against every NFL Division.

- A) True
- B) False

27) Which San Francisco head coach is the son of a former 49er head coach?

- A) Mike Nolan
- B) Ken Meyer
- C) Fred O'Connor
- D) Frank Albert

28) Who was the last 49er to lead the NFL in kickoff returns?

- A) Michael Lewis
- B) Abe Woodson
- C) Chuck Levy
- D) Joe Cribbs

29) In which decade did San Francisco have its worst winning percentage?

    A) 1950s
    B) 1960s
    C) 1970s
    D) 1980s

30) The 49ers hold the NFL league record for most penalties in a single regular season game.

    A) True
    B) False

31) What is the 49er record for most consecutive seasons leading the league in rushing?

    A) 3
    B) 5
    C) 8
    D) 10

32) Who is the only 49er Super Bowl opponent to have had a lead after the first quarter?

    A) Cincinnati Bengals
    B) Denver Broncos
    C) San Diego Chargers
    D) Miami Dolphins

Fourth Quarter
4-Point Questions

33) How many times have the 49ers led the league in total offense?

    A) 1
    B) 2
    C) 4
    D) 5

34) What is the worst defeat San Francisco has suffered in a playoff game?

    A) 28 points
    B) 33 points
    C) 42 points
    D) 46 points

35) What is the San Francisco record for consecutive regular season wins?

    A) 6
    B) 8
    C) 11
    D) 14

36) When was the last time the 49ers lead the league in passing offense?

    A) 1970
    B) 1981
    C) 1990
    D) 1995

37) How many stripes are on the sleeves of the 49ers jersey?

    A) 0
    B) 2
    C) 3
    D) 5

38) Which San Francisco QB completed the first two-point conversion in 49ers' history?

    A) Steve Young
    B) Joe Montana
    C) Jeff Garcia
    D) John Brodie

39) Who was the last San Francisco player to lead the league in total tackles?

    A) Garrison Hearst
    B) Ken Willard
    C) Kevan Barlow
    D) Patrick Willis

40) Do the 49ers have a regular season winning record against the current Super Bowl Champion New York Giants?

    A) Yes
    B) No

Fourth Quarter *4-Point Questions*

41) How big is the largest crowd to ever watch a 49ers football game at Candlestick?

    A) 64,322
    B) 65,899
    C) 66,452
    D) 69,311

42) Has a 49er running back ever had five rushing touchdowns in a single game?

    A) Yes
    B) No

43) Which of the following 49er quarterbacks NEVER had a 400-yard passing game?

    A) John Brodie
    B) Joe Montana
    C) Steve Young
    D) Jeff Garcia

44) What was the best winning percentage of a San Francisco head coach who only lasted one season or less?

    A) .167
    B) .333
    C) .571
    D) .612

45) Who was the last opponent San Francisco shutout?

- A) Atlanta Falcons
- B) Buffalo Bills
- C) Indianapolis Colts
- D) New York Giants

46) Who holds the San Francisco record for most points scored in a single season?

- A) Jerry Rice
- B) Mike Cofer
- C) Ray Wersching
- D) Gordy Soltau

47) What are the most touchdown passes by Steve Young in a single season?

- A) 22
- B) 28
- C) 36
- D) 40

48) What is the San Francisco record for most consecutive wins at home?

- A) 3
- B) 5
- C) 6
- D) 8

49) Who holds the San Francisco rushing record in the playoffs?

A) Ken Willard
B) Roger Craig
C) Billy Kilmer
D) Ricky Waters

50) How many touchdown passes did Alex Smith throw in 2007?

A) 2
B) 6
C) 9
D) 11

Fourth Quarter 49er Cool Fact

Bill Walsh was the coach who built the 49ers dynasty of the 1980s, but his legacy remains in the NFL to this day. Walsh built a scheme that included short dropbacks and novel receiving routes that later became known as the West Coast Offense. Walsh also is widely credited with inventing many of the modern basics of coaching, from the laminated sheets of plays held by coaches, to the practice of scripting the first 15 offensive plays of a game. He was named NFL Coach of the Year in 1981, and was inducted into the Pro Football Hall of Fame in 1993. Following his death on July 30, 2007, San Francisco's mayor named the 49ers' playing field the Bill Walsh Field at Monster Park. Along with this honor, the 49ers posthumously retired a jersey with the letters of his initials (BW).

Fourth Quarter Answer Key

1) A – 1986 (San Francisco tied Atlanta 10-10 in OT.)

2) D – 2007 (San Francisco lost 0-24 at Seattle.)

3) C – 10 (John Brodie [#12], Joe Montana [#16], Joe Perry [#34], Jimmy Johnson [#37], Hugh McElhenny [#39], Ronnie Lott [#42], Charlie Krueger [#70], Leo Nomellini [#73], Bob St. Clair [#79], and Dwight Clark [#87].)

4) B – No (San Francisco has led the league in both total and rushing offense in the same season on two occasions [1987 and 1998].)

5) C – Jeff Wilkins (In 1996, Wilkins completed 6 field goals which led to a 39-17 win against Atlanta.)

6) C – George Seifert (In 1989 San Francisco had a 14-2 record in the regular season which led to a 55-10 win over the Broncos in Super Bowl XXIV.)

7) D – 8 (The 49ers appeared in the playoffs every year from 1983-90.)

8) B – 1 (Bill Walsh was inducted in 1993.)

9) D – Cleveland (San Francisco has an all-time record of 7-11 against the Browns.)

10) A – Yes (Bill Walsh had a record of 4-2 against the Cowboys with a winning percentage of .667.)

11) A – Ray Brown (Ray Brown was a Consensus All-Pro in 2001 along with Terrell Owens.)

12) D – Never had two 100-yard rushers (The closest the 49ers ever came to this feat was in 2002 when Garrison Hearst rushed for 97 yards and Kevan Barlow rushed for 94 yards.)

13) A – Points scored (Cofer led the league with 121 points [27 field goals and 40 PATs].)

14) B – Garrison Hearst (Hearst gained 1,570 yards in 1998.)

15) D – Seattle (The 49ers lost 0-24 to the Seahawks in week 10 on Monday Night Football.)

16) B – False (Montana had two seasons with less than 2,000 yards [1979 with 96 yards and 1980 with 1,795 yards].)

17) B – 1948 (In 1948, fullback, Joe Perry was signed by the 49ers. He remained with the 49ers until 1950 and returned in 1963 to play his final year of football. In 1969 he was inducted into the Pro Football Hall of Fame.)

18) C – Jerry Rice (Rice had 12 seasons with over 1,000 yards [1986-96, '98].)

19) C – Billy Kilmer (In 1961, Kilmer had 10 touchdowns. In 1954 he had 4 touchdowns against Minnesota.)

20) D – Steve Young (In Young's first season as a starter he was the NFL leader in passing efficiency for the 1991 season with a 101.8 quarterback rating.)

21) C – 15 (Mike Nolan was named the 15th 49er head coach in 2005.)

22) D – 31 (In 1981 the 49ers beat the Cowboys 45-14 at home.)

23) C – Buck Shaw (Shaw went 72-37-4 from 1946-54 with a .649 winning percentage.)

24) A – Yes (The 49ers have played the Houston Texans the least amount of times, once in 2005 [1-0].)

25) B – Eric Heitmann (This award is given to a player from each team that exemplifies and displays courage.)

26) B – False (The 49ers have winning records against the NFC South, NFC East, AFC East and AFC West. They have a losing record against the AFC South and NFC West and are .500 against the NFC North and the AFC North.)

27) A – Mike Nolan (Current 49er head coach, Mike Nolan, is the son of Dick Nolan who coached the team from 1968-75.)

28) B – Abe Woodson (He led the league in 1963 with a 31.3 yard average.)

29) C – 1970s (San Francisco went 62-85-2 for a .419 winning percentage.)

30) A – True (The 49ers hold the NFL record with 22 penalties in a 1998 game against the Bills.)

31) A – 3 (San Francisco led the league in rushing for 3 consecutive seasons [1952-54].)

32) D – Miami Dolphins (Miami had a 10-7 lead after the first quarter in Super Bowl XIX. San Francisco went on to win against Miami with a score of 38-16.)

33) D – 5 (The 49ers have led in total offense 5 times [1987, 1989, 1992, 1993, and 1998].)

34) D – 46 points (The 49ers lost 3-49 to the New York Giants in the 1986 NFC Divisional Playoff at Giants Stadium.)

35) C – 11 (San Francisco won 11 straight regular season games in 1997 under Steve Mariucci.)

36) D – 1995 (The 49ers led the league twice in passing offense [1970 and 1995].)

37) C – 3 (The sleeves have three white and black stripes with the SF logo in the middle.)

38) A – Steve Young (Young completed the first two-point conversion in 49ers' history against the Philadelphia Eagles on October 2, 1994.)

39) D – Patrick Willis (Willis led the league with 174 tackles and 4 sacks in 2007.)

40) A – Yes (The 49ers are 17-15 [.531] all-time against the 2008 Super Bowl winners, the New York Giants.)

41) D – 69,311 (The 1995 NFC Divisional Playoff with the Green Bay Packers drew the largest crowd to Candlestick.)

42) B – No (In 1954 Billy Kilmer rushed for 4 touchdowns against Minnesota.)

43) A – John Brodie (Montana had 7 400-yard passing games from 1982-90, Young had 2 from 1993-95, and Garcia had 2 from 1999-2000.)

44) C – .571 (In 1976 Monte Clark finished 8-6 his only season with San Francisco.)

45) B – Buffalo Bills (The 49ers beat the Bills 35-0 in week 12 of 2001.)

46) A – Jerry Rice (Rice scored 138 points in 1987 off of 23 touchdowns.)

47) C – 36 (In 1998 Young had 36 touchdown passes with the 49ers.)

48) C – 6 (San Francisco won 6 straight games at home twice [1948 and 1992].)

49) B – Roger Craig (In the 1989 NFC Divisional Playoff against Minnesota, Craig ran for 135 yards.)

50) A – 2 (Alex started 7 games in 2007 and had one touchdown pass against Pittsburgh in week 3 and one against New Orleans in week 8.)

Note: All answers valid as of the end of the 2007 season, unless otherwise indicated in the question itself.

Overtime Bonus *4-Point Questions*

1) Which player caught the most touchdown passes thrown by Joe Montana?

   A) Freddie Solomon
   B) John Taylor
   C) Dwight Clark
   D) Jerry Rice

2) What is the longest winning streak for San Francisco in the 49ers-Rams series?

   A) 17
   B) 20
   C) 24
   D) 26

3) How many 49ers have played in 5 or more Pro Bowls?

   A) 1
   B) 4
   C) 7
   D) 10

4) San Francisco has the best playoff winning percentage in the NFL.

   A) True
   B) False

Overtime Bonus *4-Point Questions*

5) What are the most touchdown passes Joe Montana threw in a single Super Bowl?

    A) 2
    B) 3
    C) 4
    D) 5

6) Against which NFL Division does San Francisco have the best all-time winning percentage?

    A) AFC North
    B) NFC East
    C) AFC West
    D) NFC South

7) Have the 49ers ever finished the season with only one win?

    A) Yes
    B) No

8) How many 49ers have been named Pro Bowl MVP?

    A) 1
    B) 3
    C) 5
    D) 7

Overtime Bonus *4-Point Questions*

9) What position did Bill Walsh play in college?

    A) Quarterback
    B) Tackle
    C) Tight end
    D) Safety

10) What are the most points scored by San Francisco in a single game?

    A) 40
    B) 48
    C) 55
    D) 63

Overtime Bonus Answer Key

1) D – Jerry Rice (Rice has caught 55 touchdown passes from Montana. Clark is second with 41.)

2) A – 17 (Every meeting from 1990-98)

3) D – 10 (Hugh McElhenny [5], Billy Wilson [5], Jimmy Johnson [5], Guy McIntyre [5], Dave Wilcox [6], Joe Montana [7], Steve Young [7], Ronnie Lott [9], Leo Nomellini [10], and Jerry Rice [12])

4) B – False (The 49ers have a playoff record of 25-17 for a .595 winning percentage.)

5) D – 5 (Montana threw 5 touchdowns in Super Bowl XXIV for a 55-10 win over Denver.)

6) D – NFC South (111-61-3, .640 winning percentage)

7) B – No (The 49ers have finished four seasons with only two wins [1963, 1978, 1979, and 2004].)

8) B – 3 (San Francisco has had 3 players named Pro Bowl MVPs. They were Billy Wilson [1955], Hugh McElhenny [1958], and Jerry Rice [1996].)

9) C – Tight end (Bill Walsh, San Jose State, 1952-53)

10) D – 63 (In 1948 against the Brooklyn Dodgers)

Note: All answers valid as of the end of the 2007 season, unless otherwise indicated in the question itself.

Player / Team Score Sheet

Name:_____

First Quarter			Second Quarter			Third Quarter			Fourth Quarter			Overtime	
1	26		1	26		1	26		1	26		1	
2	27		2	27		2	27		2	27		2	
3	28		3	28		3	28		3	28		3	
4	29		4	29		4	29		4	29		4	
5	30		5	30		5	30		5	30		5	
6	31		6	31		6	31		6	31		6	
7	32		7	32		7	32		7	32		7	
8	33		8	33		8	33		8	33		8	
9	34		9	34		9	34		9	34		9	
10	35		10	35		10	35		10	35		10	
11	36		11	36		11	36		11	36			
12	37		12	37		12	37		12	37			
13	38		13	38		13	38		13	38			
14	39		14	39		14	39		14	39			
15	40		15	40		15	40		15	40			
16	41		16	41		16	41		16	41			
17	42		17	42		17	42		17	42			
18	43		18	43		18	43		18	43			
19	44		19	44		19	44		19	44			
20	45		20	45		20	45		20	45			
21	46		21	46		21	46		21	46			
22	47		22	47		22	47		22	47			
23	48		23	48		23	48		23	48			
24	49		24	49		24	49		24	49			
25	50		25	50		25	50		25	50			
___ x 1 =____			___ x 2 =____			___ x 3 =____			___ x 4 =____			___ x 4 =____	

Multiply total number correct by point value/quarter to calculate totals for each quarter.

Add total of all quarters below.

Total Points:_____

Thank you for playing 49erology Trivia Challenge.

Additional score sheets are available at:
www.TriviaGameBooks.com

Player / Team Score Sheet

49EROLOGY TRIVIA CHALLENGE

Name:_____

First Quarter		Second Quarter		Third Quarter		Fourth Quarter		Over
1	26	1	26	1	26	1	26	1
2	27	2	27	2	27	2	27	2
3	28	3	28	3	28	3	28	3
4	29	4	29	4	29	4	29	4
5	30	5	30	5	30	5	30	5
6	31	6	31	6	31	6	31	6
7	32	7	32	7	32	7	32	7
8	33	8	33	8	33	8	33	8
9	34	9	34	9	34	9	34	9
10	35	10	35	10	35	10	35	10
11	36	11	36	11	36	11	36	
12	37	12	37	12	37	12	37	
13	38	13	38	13	38	13	38	
14	39	14	39	14	39	14	39	
15	40	15	40	15	40	15	40	
16	41	16	41	16	41	16	41	
17	42	17	42	17	42	17	42	
18	43	18	43	18	43	18	43	
19	44	19	44	19	44	19	44	
20	45	20	45	20	45	20	45	
21	46	21	46	21	46	21	46	
22	47	22	47	22	47	22	47	
23	48	23	48	23	48	23	48	
24	49	24	49	24	49	24	49	
25	50	25	50	25	50	25	50	

___x 1 =___   ___x 2 =___   ___x 3 =___   ___x 4 =___   ___x 4 =

Multiply total number correct by point value/quarter to calculate totals for each quarter

Add total of all quarters below.

Total Points:_____

Thank you for playing 49erology Trivia Challenge.

Additional score sheets are available at:
www.TriviaGameBooks.com

87